EST. 1871

The Official
Reading
Football Club
Annual 2008

Written By Mark Bradley

A Grange Publication

© 2007. Published by Grange Communications Ltd., Edinburgh, under licence from Reading Football Club. Printed in the EU.

Editor: Mark Bradley.

Editorial assistance: Andy West.

Photography: Richard Claypole, Gareth Davies, Jason Dawson, Gary Hynard, Ian Morsman, Craig Mortimer, Nigel Smith.

© Reading Football Club.

ISBN: 978-1-906211-00-4

£6.99

CONTENTS

Welcome
to The Official Reading Football Club 2008 Annual

Last season, all our expectations were met and often exceeded. Steve Coppell, his coaching staff and his players all excelled at the highest level to carve out a glittering chapter in the Club's history by achieving a top half finish in our first ever season amongst English football's elite. We will remember our first Premier League campaign for a long time and this annual looks back at a fantastic ten months in the global limelight.

It also looks ahead to our 2007/8 challenge – one which I hope sees us set similar standards and deliver more success. I know our players will refuse to relax and be content with last season's achievements – they will strive for more and continually look to improve, whilst aiming to establish Reading FC as a force to be reckoned on the biggest stage in domestic football.

So I am greatly looking forward to another season, and I'm sure you are too! Enjoy the annual and every twist and turn this season brings us!

John Madejski OBE, DL Chairman

History is made!

The first day of the season always feels new! Fresh hope fills the stands and an unbelievable excitement, that has built over the barren football-less summer months, erupts with the first kick from the centre circle. On this occasion it felt even newer than normal as Kevin Doyle took the first touch to launch the Royals' first ever top flight campaign, making history against Middlesbrough. And it was made in the most thrillingly dramatic circumstances.

At first it seemed as though such a highly anticipated encounter would take a horrible turn for the worse. Stewart Downing returned from World Cup duties with England to calmly fire the first Premiership goal at Madejski Stadium and if the buoyant home crowd were a little shocked after the winger's opener, they were dumbstruck when Yakubu stroked Fabio Rochemback's parried free-kick past the helpless Marcus Hahnemann. Steve Coppell's men had dreamt of this day but it was turning into a nightmare.

Feet were being found though, and two minutes before the break Dave Kitson struck. Debutant Seol Ki-Hyeon weaved his way past Julio Arca and slid in a cross for Kits to stab over the line and pull one back! Hope once more! Seconds later Ivar Ingimarsson cut back a left-footed cross to Steve Sidwell, who brilliantly drilled past Mark Schwarzer and at 2-2 it was the visitors who went into the dressing rooms stunned.

Kitson didn't emerge for the second half after suffering an horrific injury in an ugly tackle from Chris Riggott, but his replacement Leroy Lita completed the comeback in fairytale fashion. Feeding off scraps from Kevin Doyle's goalmouth scramble, the £1m man powered high into the net with his left foot to signal his return from injury with a match-winning third. Mark Viduka had a late leveller ruled out for offside but the sun was shining on the Premiership's newest members, who were rightly thrust onto the front pages of sports pullouts after an immediate impact on the biggest stage.

The memories of the win would not fade for the rest of the month, despite two tight defeats.

Doyle had his first of the season within four minutes of our first away trip in the top tier, but the early lead looked fragile when Ibrahima Sonko tangled with Aston Villa's Luke Moore just inside the Royals' area. Referee Lee Mason pointed to the spot and somewhat surprisingly showed Sonks his red card, and Juan Pablo Angel beat Hahnemann from 12 yards to draw the scores level. Ten men for almost an hour was too much to ask and Gareth Barry headed the midweek winner for Villa.

Then the first week ended in disappointment with defeat at Wigan; Emile Heskey flicking home for the only goal. Lita shot straight at Chris Kirkland late on at the JJB Stadium and Reading legs were just too weary to muster another magnificent comeback.

Win, win, win and the might of United held!

He knew nothing about it when the ball hit the back of the net, but Ivar Ingimarsson had plundered three more Madejski Stadium points with a brave header beyond Manchester City's Nicky Weaver. For all Stuart Pearce's blood and thunder, it was a heroic diving header from our Icelandic centre half that began September with a bang as Sylvain Distin's forehead couldn't prevent Ivar heading home halfway through the first half.

City pressed but Sky Sports' Monday night cameras were paying their first trip to the Madejski Stadium fortress and after Ousmane Dabo's late dismissal it was Kevin Doyle, fresh from international duty in Stuttgart, who almost added to the scoreline with virtually the final kick of the game. Hatem Trabelsi slid in to clear off his own goalline but the win was Reading's and a concussed vice captain the star.

Familiar surroundings provided a welcome first away win when the two teams that topped the Championship table met at Bramall Lane for a clash of the so-called minnows. Reading, once again, left Neil Warnock with nothing to smile about – the Blades boss was down-mouthed as early as the 16th second when Doyle majestically latched onto Bobby Convey's direct pass to surge into the area and slot wide of Ian Bennett. The irrepressible Seol lasered a second soon after and despite Rob Hulse's narrow-angled near post consolation, the Royals held on to secure bragging rights over their newly-promoted colleagues and record their first ever top flight win away from home!

The distraction of the cup was almost very fleeting as a much-changed Reading line-up just scraped through an opening Carling Cup tie with League Two Darlington. Leroy Lita stumbled across some slack defensive work to drive low past David Stockdale twice, but Julian Joachim rolled back the years to match the Royals striker with two of his own and, having opened the scoring from the spot, the Quakers led no less than three times. But debutant defender Peter Mate bundled home an 86th minute equaliser with part-thigh, part-hand, and the tie went to extra time. Darlington's ten men

held on for penalties but the drama wasn't over: Stephen Hunt was allowed to re-take his 12-yarder and duly converted, and although spotkick king Doyle saw his strike saved, inaccuracies from the visitors and Andre Bikey's decisive strike smoothed the home side's path into the Third Round.

After such a low-profile clash, Steve Coppell's side were rewarded with the glamour of hosting Manchester United in the Premiership four days later. Sir Alex's side had just been upset by Arsenal at Old Trafford and pundits predicted a backlash. It never came and a second defeat for the champions elect was only avoided through the sheer brilliance of the PFA's Player of the Season. Gary Neville had no arguments after the referee pointed to the spot soon after the interval; Graeme Murty's cross had struck his opposite number's right arm and Doyle remained calm to squeeze his penalty under Edwin van der Sar. Reading were deservedly winning against Manchester United – you needed to pinch yourself! Cristiano Ronaldo needed just an inch of space and a glimpse of goal to lash a leveller past Marcus Hahnemann, but a point against such esteemed opponents offered even the most doubting of fans reason to believe we belonged amongst the elite.

Thrills and spills as emotion runs high

Encounters with ex-boss Alan Pardew had been feisty affairs in years gone by, but after a torrential downpour prior to kick off and a second minute stunner from Seol Ki-Hyeon the clash with West Ham was a relatively calm affair, though the 1-0 Upton Park win was not without last gasp incident. Evading the puddles on the pitch, our South Korean star found the top left corner with a powerful drive that separated the teams but inside injury time Yossi Benayoun ghosted in between defenders to stab a lob over Marcus Hahnemann only for Steve Sidwell's desperately arched frame to somehow head the Israeli midfielder's effort safe from underneath his own crossbar and secure victory!

Chelsea's visit was highly anticipated but the day the champions came to town was marred by two injuries to two goalkeepers and all the aftermath that followed. Winger Stephen Hunt hit the headlines for an accidental collision with Petr Cech, leaving the Czech stopper seriously hurt and Jose Mourinho understandably upset but irrationally irate. From that opening minute, every tackle was whole-heartedly contested and every ball chased down with vim and vigour. But the result swung on an inconceivably unfortunate deflection as Frank Lampard's driven free kick cannoned off Ivar Ingimarsson's leg to evade Hahnemann's dive. Both sides had a man sent off, a scuffle on the touchline blew over and John Terry donned the gloves for the final minutes after Carlo Cudicini suffered concussion in desperately defending his side's slender lead. Chelsea had clung to three points, and they celebrated bare-chested as if they'd won the World Cup, but what an eventful afternoon!

The big names and big games came thick and fast, and a similarly gutsy clash was expected when the Arsenal team coach pulled up outside Madejski Stadium's doors. But the Royals were simply outplayed by a slick Gunners outfit. The football was breathtakingly brilliant at times and Thierry Henry ended a 1051-minute shut-out to slot home an early opener in front of the previously impregnable North Stand. Alexander Hleb and Robin Van Persie stylishly added to the advantage and Henry added his second of the afternoon from the spot. Unlike against United or Chelsea, Reading had been ruthlessly exposed by Arsene's men.

The Royals' first ever trip to Anfield pitted the two teams together in the Carling Cup, and another thriller began. Three goals in six minutes catapulted Liverpool into a seemingly unassailable lead, but Bikey scored his first goal in blue and white hoops to pull one back. Peter Crouch beat the offside trap to sidefoot the hosts 4-1 ahead, but goals from Leroy Lita and Shane Long had Liverpool hearts in mouths as Reading's 'never-say-die' attitude produced the Anfield faithful with an anxious final five minutes. But the cup adventure came to an end as time ran out and the Royals had to prepare for a trip to the south coast when Premiership action resumed.

That preparation was not enough to prevent a high-flying Portsmouth side earning more plaudits with a 3-1 win at Fratton Park. Kanu pressured Brynjar Gunnarsson into a near post own goal before adding a second himself. Pedro Mendes then brilliantly volleyed a third before preventing a comeback goal at the other end by saving Gunnarsson's header with his hand. He could do nothing about Kevin Doyle's consolation but the fightback came too little and too late.

Spurs slip up and winning ways return!

Reading's second trip to Anfield – just ten days after the first – could only muster the same outcome. Liverpool had never hosted the Royals before this season and now, in Steve Coppell's second visit, the Reds had beaten their Berkshire-based challengers in both cup and league battles. Dirk Kuyt failed to notch in Madejski Stadium's pre-season curtain raiser – his Feyenoord side lost 2-1 to the Royals in early August – but this time the Dutch international bagged a brace to end Reading's resistance and condemn Coppell's side to a fifth game without a win.

The rotten run came to an end a week later with a glittering win against Martin Jol's inconsistent Spurs. Despite stunning form in the Uefa Cup, an excellent 2-1 victory over Chelsea, and a lead given to them by Robbie Keane from the penalty spot, Reading were ready to give Spurs an uncomfortable away day. Nicky Shorey swerved a sweetly struck 25-yarder wide of Paul Robinson's left palm to level and both Kevin Doyle and Steve Sidwell were left alone from a corner soon after for the latter to stab the hosts into the lead before the break. Jermain Defoe could and maybe should have restored parity with just more than 10 minutes left, and he was made to pay for his wayward effort when Doyle sped onto Hahnemann's quick restart, burst past Ledley King and drove across Robinson to seal the points. An Arsenal fan (Shorey), an ex-Arsenal player (Sidwell) and Robbie Keane's Irish international colleague (Doyle) had poetically put Tottenham in their place.

Confidence was fully restored and that showed when Charlton became another London side to be put to the sword. Les Reed was still wet behind the ears in management

terms and he learned a lot from how little his Addicks side challenged the Royals in a comfortable 2-0 home win.

18 minutes in and Shorey's pinpoint cross was asking to be headed home – Seol gladly obliged. 18 minutes from the end and Steve Sidwell's miscued swipe span into Doyle's path – not needing a second invitation the free-scoring striker placed the points in the bag.

Fulham found themselves next in line to defend the capital's honour but the Royals took another three points from Craven Cottage courtesy of a stonewall penalty decision that left the Lilywhites with ten men for much of the match. Ian Pearce's lunge was rash and Kevin Doyle's path to goal was blocked by the centre back's legs, so the Irishman added to Fulham's red card woes by getting to his feet to calmly convert from the spot. The hosts lay siege to Marcus Hahnemann's goal for lengthy spells but the back line remained strong and repelled waves of attacks. This Premiership lark looked easy!

Dream trips earn Royals' respect!

Kevin Doyle's name stood alongside that of Didier Drogba's as the top flight's top scorers chart took shape. And the Irishman's eighth of the season was enough to deny Bolton any reward from their trip south. John Oster's first start of the campaign saw the wing wizard make an immediate impact with the crucial assist and Doyle's nodded finish took Reading into sixth with a 1-0 win, drawing the newest Premiership members level on points with Arsenal!

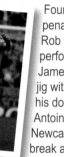

Four days later a controversial penalty decision from referee Rob Styles ruined an inspired performance at St James' Park. James Harper danced a merry jig with kit man Ron Grant after his double strike cancelled out Antoine Sibierski's opener and Newcastle looked clueless after the break as the Royals took control... until the man in the middle adjudged Obafemi Martins' tumble over Ibrahima Sonko's hip to be authentic. The Nigerian struck the penalty past Hahnemann and late on Emre rubbed salt into Royals' wounds by unleashing an unstoppable 22-yard effort that fizzed through the US stopper's hands.

A less arduous motorway trip to Watford followed, but little glee came for either team from an encounter that according to past meetings was always destined to end in a hard-fought goalless draw.

Back at home and the promise of six points before Christmas was realistic. Blackburn were struggling to find consistency and when Harper laced up his goalscoring boots once again with a 41st minute finish it looked like being enough. But Benni McCarthy tried, tried and tried and eventually beat the offside trap to get one of his goals written in ink on the scoresheet. In the dying stages, David Bentley capitalised on space down Blackburn's right and his bullet made it 2-1 to Rovers.

With trips to Chelsea and Manchester United looming very large, Everton's pre-Christmas visit was unproductive. Andy Johnson scored, as always against Reading, and James McFadden put the game beyond the Royals reach as Steve Coppell's side had to swallow their turkey with the prospect of another thunderous clash with the Blues on their minds.

Although the stormy Stamford Bridge reception was intimidating for a while on Boxing Day, the Reading players refused to lower their levels of self-expectation. When Didier Drogba leapt high to head home Frank Lampard's corner Blues fans sensed revenge for Petr Cech's absence. But ex-Chelsea youngster Leroy Lita brilliantly headed past Hilario to exact some of his own retribution on his former club. Drogba struck once more before Ashley Cole and Michael Essien conspired to put a routine clearance over their own goal line and Reading had deservedly taken a precious Premiership point from the champions!

By holding their closest rivals, Reading had done their next opponents Manchester United a big favour. But Steve Coppell's men walked out at Old Trafford brimming with belief. And although the table toppers took all three points, in the dying stages the United masses were whistling nervously for injury time to elapse. Ole Gunnar Solskjaer started the scoring but Ibrahima Sonko rose highest to glance home an equaliser before half time. Ryan Giggs came off the bench as the home side started to worry and Cristiano Ronaldo fired inside both posts to establish a two-goal cushion. Sam Sodje had seen red as he tried to shackle Wayne Rooney, but Leroy Lita rose to the occasion again to fire Reading back into it late on. Another dramatic late equaliser wasn't to be though, and United had escaped unscathed.

Goals galore!

New Year's Day was one for West Ham to forget! At the end of a 6-0 drubbing, the biggest win of the top flight season belonged to Reading! Brynjar Gunnarsson elegantly glanced home the first and Stephen Hunt bagged the second before wheeling away to complete a weird, wild yet wonderful touchline celebration. All good thrashings include a deflating own goal and Anton Ferdinand became the culprit only for Kevin Doyle to fire a fourth before the break. Leroy Lita and Doyle's second sent the sorry East Londoners home exasperated, in shock and full of woe. The Royals had begun the year in scintillating form.

It almost seemed a waste to apply such momentum to an FA Cup clash with Burnley, but a rain-delayed 3-2 victory – courtesy of Leroy Lita, Shane Long and Sam Sodje – allowed Dave Kitson a long-awaited return to action and set up another tie with Birmingham later in the month. The same scoreline was secured at St Andrews, with Kitson's third minute swivel and strike starting the action before Lita's impressive brace meant Martin Taylor's strike and Sebastian Larsson's last gasp free kick weren't enough to halt the Royals' path into relatively uncharted cup territory.

Meanwhile, two Premiership fixtures had taken place with two men taking top billing whilst Reading remained unbeaten. Before kick off at Goodison Park, Sylvester Stallone strode out to the centre circle with thousands of fans, players, press and officials applauding in awe. Promoting the new 'Rocky' film and his new found allegiance to Everton, Sly completely upstaged the Premiership fixture that followed – for the record Stephen Hunt's header

was clumsily deflected over his own goal line by Joleon Lescott to earn the Royals the lead but Andy Johnson's inevitable equaliser secured a draw.

Back at Madejski Stadium it was Mr Neil Warnock who unsurprisingly drew all the attention. His stamping gesture on the touchline was not appreciated by Royals coach Wally Downes and a scuffle between the two benches threatened to overshadow another comfortable win over the Blades. It didn't; Shane Long scored his first top flight goal, Ulises De La Cruz bagged his first in Reading colours with a fantastic solo run, and after Hunt had been on the receiving end of a violent elbow from the quickly-dismissed Keith Gillespie, the Irishman acrobatically added a third.

There was still time in a fixture-filled opening month of the year to deny Wigan a second success of the season. Emile Heskey threatened to be the matchwinner again with a sweetly struck third minute opener, but Ivar Ingimarsson headed into a goalmouth vacated by a wandering Chris Kirkland, Shane Long rose above David Unsworth to do the same after the break, and Lita capitalised on a loose ball that spiralled away from a collision between Kirlkand and Kitson to tidily put the result beyond doubt. Five wins and a draw from January!

The tale of two cup-ties

Leroy Lita had just been recalled to the international scene after Stuart Pearce picked the Royals goal-getter in his first England under-21 squad. But Manchester City's manager was given a sour taste of what the Reading striker had to offer only days before the under-21 clash with Spain. The £1m man had already seen a good goal harshly ruled out in the first half, but undeterred he smashed a fantastic strike past Andreas Isaksson to break the deadlock in the 79th minute. That finish was matched by a driven second two minutes from time and Royals fans celebrated three more points in the low fog descending upon the City of Manchester Stadium.

Another 2-0 scoreline followed seven days later in an early afternoon kick off at Madejski Stadium. Aston Villa had benefited from Ibrahima Sonko's red card earlier in the season, but the injured centre back was able to watch Reading reap some revenge on Martin O'Neill's outfit. Steve Sidwell stole the show, ghosting in at the near post to glance home Stephen Hunt's corner and then elegantly linking up with

Dave Kitson to collect a return ball and effortlessly sidefoot wide of Thomas Sorensen and seal victory.

Less enchanting trips to Burnley and Birmingham led Steve Coppell's side into a glamorous fixture at Old Trafford in the Fifth Round of the FA Cup, and just as the Royals had held Manchester United to a league 1-1 draw at Madejski Stadium, now they repeated the feat in the cup thanks to Brynjar Gunnarsson's second half header that flew high into the net to cancel out Michael Carrick's long-range drive. Adam Federici's dad had flown over from Australia to see his son in action at the Theatre of Dreams, and the Aussie stopper didn't disappoint by producing a spectacular tie-saving fingertip touch to turn Henrik Larsson's effort wide and force a replay.

Sandwiched in between the United cup clashes came a trip to Middlesbrough, but it was fast forgotten. The class of Mark Viduka told and together with his prolific strike partner Yakubu, Gareth Southgate's were propelled into a 2-0 lead. This time no dramatic comeback looked likely, even though John Oster pulled one back towards the end.

The highly-anticipated cup replay started less heroically for Federici; Gabriel Heinze's 22-yard drive squirming under the keeper's frame and for a second minute lead. It got worse...a lot worse...quickly, as Louis Saha and Ole Gunnar Solskjaer powered two more past the helpless Royals goalkeeper, and Reading were startled – three down in six minutes! Evasive action saw the Royals revert to their more familiar 4-4-2 formation and Kitson nodded home to ease fears of a cricket score. Suddenly the contest was back on. Steve Coppell's side were dominant but couldn't find a second until six minutes from time; Leroy Lita brilliantly directing a diving header past Edwin Van der Sar. Gunnarsson came inches away from true hero's status but his last gasp thunderbolt battered the crossbar and the Wembley dream came to an end with a 3-2 defeat. But Reading could be proud of their players.

Fixture-free frustration

Having been bombarded with seven games in December, six in January and five more in February, football fans were left desperate for more from March. Due to an international break and a weekend set aside for the FA Cup quarter finals, Reading only had two games scheduled in a very quiet month. The first of those grabbed the attention – away at Arsenal's pristine new stadium. James Harper and Steve Sidwell returned to their former club but sampled the Emirates environment for the first time, and although the Gunners deserved their 2-1 victory, the latter of the two ex-Arsenal midfielders came so close to clinching a point late on.

The Gunners' trip to Berkshire had left locals singing their praises, and again Arsene Wenger's men were demonstrating their brand of swift and stylish football. Cesc Fabregas squandered an open goal and Marcus Hahnemann pushed the Spaniard's long-range effort over to keep the game goalless, but Andre Bikey was deceived by Gael Clichy's deadly pace and conceded a penalty. Gilberto made no mistake and soon after Julio Baptista powered through the Royals back line to double the advantage. Characteristically the Royals earned a late lifeline when Fabregas did find the net...his own!

And Sidwell's well-struck drive was brilliantly kept out by Jens Lehmann at his near post to deny the midfielder a dream return.

Two football-starved weeks later Portsmouth were the visitors, and with such long gaps between games the home crowd were desperate for something to cheer. They got the opposite as Madejski Stadium played host to its only goalless draw of the season. A pair of stubborn defences dominated, so much so that it was a Pompey centre half that came closest to scoring for the Royals – Linvoy Primus muscling Leroy Lita off the ball only to stab perilously toward the bottom left corner of his own goal. Resorting to strikes from distance, Pompey's Richard Hughes came dangerously close in the dying stages but his 30-yard rasper cannoned off the crossbar and away to safety. But all efforts to find a breakthrough were in vain.

The international interval provided little rest for some of the Royals stars. The most glittering contributions came from our Irish trio – all playing a part in Steve Staunton's side for crucial qualifying wins against Wales and Slovakia. Kevin Doyle scored the only goal to beat the Eastern Europeans, while Stephen Hunt and Shane Long made their international bows in impressive style. And Leroy Lita made a trip to the brand new Wembley Stadium, playing well in a 3-3 tussle with Italy. Even better news came back at Reading as Steve Coppell, the man who has masterminded the Royals' passage into the Premiership, signed a new two-year contract to the delight of all involved.

The race for Europe ignites!

Spurs had been the victims of Reading's most impressive victory at Madejski Stadium earlier in the season, but full debutant Greg Halford literally handed Martin Jol's side three points in the return clash. The travelling support thought Alan Wiley was playing some sort of cruel April Fools prank when he pointed the spot to give Robbie Keane his second chance of the season to convert past Marcus Hahnemann from 12 yards. True, the ball had skipped up and brushed the hand of the Royals' record signing on the very edge of the area, but it was unintentional without a doubt – despite protestations the penalty kick stood, Keane made no mistake, and three points went to Spurs.

Liverpool boss Rafael Benitez's rotational policy had come under scrutiny throughout the season and as the final stages of the Champions League approached his league line-ups were becoming increasingly hard to forecast, but it was two changes he made in the second half that conjured a win for his side in Reading. Alvaro Arbeloa had caught the home side cold with a stunning breakaway move that was beautifully finished by the Spanish left back, before Brynjar Gunnarsson's penchant for the big stage again proved profitable when he surged forward from right back to lash a fantastic effort past Jose Reina to level. But two of Benitez's substitutes combined as Jermaine Pennant crossed for Dirk Kuyt to strike at the far post and there was no time for another comeback.

There were only two days to reflect on that unlucky loss before an Easter Monday trip to a resurgent Charlton. While Steve Coppell was half hoping for a European berth, Alan Pardew was eking his side towards unlikely safety, but despite the passion on show the deadlock could not be broken and a goalless draw helped neither team.

Contrasting to the Addicks' positive mental attitude, Fulham then arrived in Berkshire in relative chaos and with a new manager desperate to make an early impact. Photographers swarmed around Lawrie Sanchez before the crucial clash against his former side but Stephen Hunt struck early to transform the new boss' smile into an effortless look of angst. Papa Bouba Diop had a legitimate equaliser ruled out for offside and Michael Brown slammed a late strike against the crossbar in bad luck indicative of a side struggling to survive, and Reading clung to the win that ended a barren run.

Then came a trip to Bolton, which became one of the most memorable games of a season containing so many highs. The two teams cancelled each other out until Nicky Shorey slid in to deflect a wayward Nicolas Anelka effort into an unguarded net. There seemed to be no way back but a triple substitution breathed new life into the Royals' late surge. Kevin Doyle fully punished Abdoulaye Meite for an unnecessary late lunge by converting from the spot, and before there was time to reflect on whether a 1-1 was a fair result, the Royals fans were deliriously celebrating a second from their Irish striker. Incredibly then it was 3-1 when Stephen Hunt headed Shorey's sublime cross past Jussi Jaaskelainen – from nothing the Royals had earned a flattering victory that truly threw Reading's name back into the reckoning for a European qualification berth!

At the end of the month Michael Owen's comeback was upstaged by Dave Kitson's drilled finish, and three more points against Newcastle did the Royals' Uefa Cup push no harm at all. The race was still on!

Last day drama – a fitting end!

Despite Steve Coppell's often repeated uncertainty, it seemed as though a place in Europe was fatefully written in Reading's stars. The Royals had revelled in proving their critics wrong at every turn and victory at Bolton had started supporters scouring the remaining fixture lists for Uefa Cup contenders; Spurs had games in hand and a relatively comfortable run-in, but Bolton, Everton and Portsmouth all had tricky ties against some of the league's best. With a home clash against already relegated Watford next up for Coppell's men, everyone expected three points. None came.

The hosts failed to capitalise on their total dominance and paid the ultimate price when Danny Shittu sprung the offside trap from a free kick to tap home unchallenged and gift the rock-bottom Hornets the lead. Startled and somewhat deflated Royals stars fought desperately for a way back but Marlon King nodded a second past Marcus Hahnemann from close range and Reading had been beaten. It was a sorry end to the Madejski Stadium campaign, and the lap of honour that richly deserved high praise from the home support was applauded a little half-heartedly as the reality of the result sunk in.

There was still hope as Blackburn stood in Reading's way on the final day of the season. Rovers couldn't catch Coppell's men but had their own agenda; Mark Hughes' side needed victory to guarantee themselves a spot in the pre-season Inter Toto Cup. The Royals needed to better Bolton's result and hope Arsenal kept Portsmouth quiet. The Gunners did their job – a goalless draw at Fratton Park kept Pompey out of the reckoning. Spurs leapfrogged already Europe-bound Everton with a win over Manchester City, enabling them to clinch fifth spot.

Bolton faced Aston Villa and in a topsy-turvy tussle, Sammy Lee scraped his first point in a 2-2 draw against Martin O'Neill's mid-tablers. A win, therefore, would have meant seventh place belonged to Reading. But in a thrilling climax at Ewood Park, Reading never led.

If Benni McCarthy's tap in had been ruled out for a foul by Shabani Nonda on the crumpled Marcus Hahnemann it might have been different. But it wasn't, and Seol Ki-Hyeon had to equalise with a far post header. If Morten Gamst Pedersen's close range stab had rebounded off the left upright anywhere other than at David Bentley's feet, it might have given Kevin Doyle's header two minutes later an added importance. But Bentley tapped home. If Matt Derbyshire's introduction from the bench had come just a minute later, his first touch might not have been a headed finish from Brett Emerton's cross. Gunnarsson's outstanding snapshot drive levelled in emphatic style soon after. And if Ivar Ingimarsson's glanced near post header had not been ruled out for a push, passports would have been at the ready.

One goal, a winning goal, would have ended Reading's season with a Uefa Cup place. The ifs and buts went against the Royals on the final afternoon, but upon the final whistle everyone associated with the Club overflowed with pride in applauding Reading's astonishing achievements in their first season amongst English football's elite.

Ever Present

Ivar Ingimarsson keen to repeat mammoth season-long effort

"I was delighted to put pen to paper on a new deal in the summer. Now I can look forward to the next three years here at Reading. I don't like moving around and leaving Reading has never occurred to me. Me and my family are really settled here, we really like our life here and we don't want to go anywhere else. And they must have thought I'd done enough to deserve a new and longer contract." If playing in every minute of every match is not sufficient commitment for the Club, then surely we are asking too much of players. Ivar was voted the Royals 'Player of the season' in Reading's first top flight league season after skippering the side on no fewer than 15 occasions, helping keep 13 clean sheets at the back, scoring twice (the only goal against Manchester City and the opener in a win over Wigan), whilst spending more than 57 hours on the pitch. But he's ready to start all over again for Steve Coppell's side.

"... so far in every season I have felt fitter than I have in the one before."

Our Icelandic international celebrates his 30th birthday only eight days after our Old Trafford curtain raiser, but Ivar is feeling fitter than ever and has no complaints about the workload he was given last season. "My new deal gives me another three years and after that we'll just have to see – I'll be coming up to being an old man! I've always tried to be fitter and better each year and so far in every season I have felt fitter than I have in the one before. That is my

Minutes played in the Premier League in 2006/7 (including injury time)

1	Phil Jagielka (Sheffield United)	3662
2	Joseph Yobo (Everton)	3656
3	David James (Portsmouth)	3654
4	Ivar Ingimarsson (Reading)	3647
5	Jussi Jaaskelainen (Bolton)	3646
6	Richard Dunne (Man City)	3644
7	Paul Robinson (Tottenham)	3639
8	Liam Rosenior (Fulham)	3630
9	Brad Friedel (Blackburn)	3608
10	Lee Carsley (Everton)	3583

Outfield players who played in every Premier League match in 2006/7

Gabriel Agbonlahor (Aston Villa)

Lee Carsley (Everton)

Richard Dunne (Man City)

Cesc Fabregas (Arsenal)

James Harper (Reading)

Ivar Ingimarsson (Reading)

Phil Jagielka (Sheffield United)

Joleon Lescott (Everton)

Brian McBride (Fulham)

Olof Mellberg (Aston Villa)

Liam Rosenior (Fulham)

Gary Speed (Bolton)

Joseph Yobo (Everton)

"He is always one to stay behind at training and as a result he didn't miss a game."

me. Now we have to stop people talking about 'the second season syndrome.' Hopefully here at Reading we can show that that doesn't apply to us."

Royals boss Steve Coppell is confident Ivar can reach the same high standards he set himself last season with more influential displays from the back. "We had a few contenders for player of the season last season - a few people who have been critical to what we did. Ivar was captain many times and he remains such a great professional. He is always one to stay behind at training and as a result he didn't miss a game. He didn't even have a break when others did, because he is a regular for Iceland so is kept busy on international weekends. It's a huge compliment to him."

But can he win the Player of the Season award for a second season running? It's not on the Icelander's agenda. "I'm not thinking about being player of the season again. You go into a

aim again this season."
As the first signing Steve Coppell made as Royals boss, Ivar has been with Reading throughout their recent rise to the Premier League, and even when he joined Ivar felt that this Club was making progress towards English football's elite. "When I first arrived, I thought that this was a club that was going places and that has proven to be the case. I think the first year in the Premier League was always going to be a trial season for many of our players...including

Clean sheets kept in 2006/7

1 Chelsea 22

2 Liverpool 20

3 Manchester United 16

4 Everton 14

5 Manchester City 14

6 Aston Villa 13

7 Reading 13

8 Arsenal 12

9 Bolton 12

10 Portsmouth 12

Past 'Player of the Season' winners

2006/7 - Ivar Ingimarsson

2005/6 - Kevin Doyle

2004/5 - Dave Kitson

2003/4 - Graeme Murty

2002/3 - James Harper

2001/2 - Graeme Murty

season trying to do well and more importantly trying to help the team doing well. That is the only goal and hopefully I can be a big part of some more success in our second season in the Premier League too."

Royals Quiz see page 60 for answers

The 2006/7 Season

August: Which player made his Royals debut by starting in a 1-0 defeat at Wigan's JJB Stadium in the opening week of the season?

September: Which Reading player saw his spotkick legitimately saved in our Carling Cup penalty shootout win over Darlington?

October: Can you name the four substitutes that sat on the bench in Reading's first ever trip to Anfield but didn't play a part in our 4-3 Carling Cup defeat to Liverpool?

November: Who was felled by Ibrahima Sonko to earn Robbie Keane a penalty-kick in a 3-1 Royals win over Spurs?

December: Ashley Cole clumsily cleared but it cannoned off Michael Essien and over the Chelsea goalline. Reading were level at Stamford Bridge on Boxing Day but which Royals player provided the troublesome cross for that equaliser?

January: Which player scored the first goal of the new year; one of six in the biggest top flight victory all season?

February: John Oster's late consolation at Middlesbrough was the winger's first Premiership goal since scoring the fourth in a 4-2 win over Barnsley in September 1997! Who was our midfield star playing for at the time?

March: Both Arsenal goalscorers in a 2-1 Royals defeat at the new Emirates Stadium were of the same nationality. Which country do they belong to?

April: Who netted the only goal in our 1-0 home win over Fulham?

May: Adam Federici had to replace the injured Marcus Hahnemann in the first half of our final day draw against Blackburn Rovers. In which other league game did the Aussie stopper emerge from the bench to cover for the crocked Royals no.1?

The Opposition

1. Besides Dave Kitson, which other player suffered a first half injury to force his half-time withdrawal in the Royals' astonishing opening day win against Middlesbrough?

2. Which player went unpunished despite handballing on his own goalline to prevent Brynjar Gunnarsson's header creeping over the line in our 3-1 defeat at Portsmouth?

3. Which four opposition players scored in their own net in Premiership fixtures against Reading in 2006/7?

4. Which Manchester City player was sent off in our 1-0 win over the Blues at Madejski Stadium in September?

5. Which two players top scored against the Royals with three goals apiece in Premier League clashes against Steve Coppell's side?

Season's End

1. Which player followed his successful promotion-winning season with the Royals by clinching a second consecutive league title at another club in 2006/7?

2. Can you name the two Reading players involved in end-of-season playoff challenges as part of loan spells?

3. Who became the first new signing of the summer after the season's end?

4. Against which team did Madejski Stadium see its highest attendance record set?

5. Kevin Doyle was nominated for the prestigious PFA Young Player of the Year award... alongside which five other players?

Internationals

1. Kevin Doyle and Shane Long scored their first international goals for Republic of Ireland in 2006/7 – against which two teams did they open their respective accounts?

2. Nicky Shorey's call-up to the full England squad came in late May after first pulling on the three lions shirt for a 'B' international days earlier. Who was that 'B' game against, what was the score and where was it played?

3. Which Reading player featured in this summer's Copa America tournament?

4. Which player, having not featured in Steve Coppell's first team since his move to Reading, played a significant part under Steve Staunton when the Republic of Ireland toured South America?

5. Which player was on the winning side on the opening day of Reading's season after finishing his last competitive match on the losing side in a World Cup Finals defeat to Switzerland?

Trivia

1. Which three Royals players were shown Premiership red cards in the club's first top flight season?

2. Ivar Ingimarsson played every minute of our first Premier League campaign – which three outfield players at other clubs achieved the same feat?

3. Which Royals player finished the season with the best goals-per-minutes ratio?

4. Can you name the three players who wore the Reading FC captain's armband?

5. There were ten penalties taken across all competitions in Royals games in 2006/7 and all were converted! But what percentage were Reading spotkicks stroked home by Kevin Doyle?

Name that Player

Show your support ...
Join the
Young Royals

You will receive an exclusive membership pack with fantastic Reading FC goodies
Plus – enter Young Royals competitions for the chance to win amazing prizes including

★ Reading FC items signed by the team
★ Meet the players at special members only events
★ Watch First Team training sessions
★ Lead the Royals out as a mascot onto the Madejski Stadium pitch

Join now for only £10 for the 2007/8 season

How to join
In person – visit the Sales Centre at Madejski Stadium (Mon-Fri 10am-6pm)
Online – download an application form from the Young Royals page on www.readingfc.co.uk and post to the Sales Centre

Marcus Hahnemann

Shorey for England!!

Loyal Royals were starting to wonder whether their persistent chants were falling on deaf ears. For years the words 'Shorey for England' have echoed around Madejski Stadium's four stands imploring Sven Goran Eriksson, and now Steve McClaren, to sit up and take notice of our consistently brilliant left back. And after an excellent display for England 'B' against Albania, long-awaited international recognition arrived the following day; Nicky Shorey was named in the full England squad for a friendly against the might of Brazil and a crucial European Championships qualifier in Estonia.

"I'm just delighted, I can't really believe it! It will probably only be when we meet up and I start training with the lads that it will sink in," he told the Royals' official website immediately after receiving the call-up.

"The Brazil game couldn't be a better showpiece for the new Wembley Stadium, and I'm sure everyone in England will be tuning in to watch so it will be a great experience for me to be involved in.

"From my point of view it will just be nice to go out and train with players of that stature. But really it all just leads up to the all-important game in Estonia, which is one we have to win."

Typically, Shorey's impact was underplayed and somewhat lost in the headline-grabbing story that told the tale of David Beckham's return to the fold. And as the cameras frantically flashed every time the ex-England skipper stood over the ball, the Royals full back quietly produced an impressively assured performance in the

AN FA ENGLAND INTERNATIONAL MATCH

ENGLAND v BRAZIL

WEMBLEY STADIUM

FRIDAY, 1 JUNE 2007
KICK OFF 20:00HRS

ENGLAND	BRAZIL
1 Paul ROBINSON (GK)	1 HELTON (GK)
2 Jamie CARRAGHER	2 Daniel ALVES
3 Nicky SHOREY	3 NALDO
4 Steven GERRARD	4 JUAN
5 Ledley KING	5 MINEIRO
6 John TERRY (C)	6 GILBERTO
7 David BECKHAM	7 RONALDINHO
8 Frank LAMPARD	8 Gilberto SILVA (C)
9 Alan SMITH	9 Vagner LOVE
10 Michael OWEN	10 KAKÁ
11 Joe COLE	11 ROBINHO

Substitutes	Substitutes
12 Wes BROWN	12 DONI (GK)
13 Scott CARSON (GK)	13 MAICON
14 Wayne BRIDGE	14 Alex SILVA
15 Phil NEVILLE	15 ALEX
16 Michael CARRICK	16 MARCELO
17 Jermaine JENAS	17 EDMILSON
18 David BENTLEY	18 JOSUÉ
19 Kieron DYER	19 ELANO
20 Stewart DOWNING	20 DIEGO
21 Peter CROUCH	21 AFONSO
22 Robert GREEN (GK)	22 JÔ
23 Jermain DEFOE	

Manager	Manager
Steve McCLAREN	DUNGA

Referee	Assistant Referees	Fourth Official
Markus MERK (Germany)	Fernando TAMAYO (Ecuador) Saleh Mohamed AL MARZOUQI (UAE)	Daniel BENNETT (South Africa)

first international at the new Wembley Stadium.

88,745 people saw Shorey become the first Reading player to play for England in more than a century – Herbert Smith was the last to pull on the shirt in 1904/5 – and confidently he shackled Kaka and Ronaldinho as one of only four outfield players to play the full 90 minutes.

He seemed immediately at home on the biggest stage under maximum scrutiny and the fiercest glare of the media spotlight. "It was amazing," he revealed in the frenzied media 'mixed zone' after the 1-1 draw. "To make my debut, against Brazil... it was something else!

"When we walked out for the national anthem it was unbelievable. I've always dreamed of that moment and to do that today in front of 90,000 people...the hairs on the back of my neck were definitely standing up!

"I was a bit nervous, but the lads all calmed me down, so it was good and I thought it went alright. A few passes went astray but I really enjoyed it."

Again Shorey's debut display was largely overlooked in the post-match papers, swamped by plaudits for Beckham, but the cultured left-footer can only be pleased with his England bow. The mentions he did receive in the media all lauded his input and no questions were raised about his capability at international level. He had made it and more is sure to come for the model of defensive consistency.

The Friday fixture came less than 24 hours before another big day in Nicky's life – his wedding! Before flying out to link up with England again for a vital tie in Tallinn, Shorey completed a wonderful weekend by marrying his fiancee Emily. Glen Little, Graeme Murty and former Royal Steve Sidwell were among the guests but with three lions awaiting him in Eastern Europe, the honeymoon was understandably put on hold!

It certainly wasn't Sweden! In previous preseason trips, Steve Coppell and his men have opted to spend short fortnights in small hotels stranded in rural Scandinavia, playing games against lowly non-league amateurs and romping to double figures scorelines in an attempt to prime themselves for the coming season. This year, the Peace Cup came calling and a trip to one of most densely populated areas of the world was promised. Drawn in a group with River Plate from Argentina, Olympique Lyonnais from France and a Japanese side called Shimizu S-Pulse, competition was going to be of the highest calibre and was set to be played out in impressive stadia built to host the World Cup five years ago. This would be an experience like none other for the Royals.

Day One: **Tuesday, 10th July 2007**

At 5pm on Monday, sliding away from a sleepy Madejski Stadium on a balmy Berkshire evening, Reading began their Peace Cup adventure. At 5pm [South Korean time] the following afternoon, there wasn't much calmness about the Royals' arrival in Seoul. After a 10-hour flight, the dim glimmer of a reading light in business class was suddenly swapped for the flashing cameras at the Arrivals Lounge. Reading were making front page headlines in the Far East without kicking a ball.

words Seol Ki-Hyeon had been mentioned, her eyes had lit up! Seol is a star here and was meeting up with the rest of the squad at the hotel. The Royals were sure to make a lot of friends in two weeks.

After kit man Ron Grant had managed to drag all the kit bags off the luggage lounge conveyor belt and onto trolleys, it was time to traipse out to the coach. Cameramen, photographers, journalists and Asian-based loyal Royals swarmed around the Reading players in a controlled but frantic media huddle. A photoshoot took place with some of the more sleepy plane passengers struggling to muster much of a smile, but Steve Coppell and Kevin Doyle answered questions via a translator in the middle of the scrum while a number of security men watched on.

The coach journey to the hotel brought a little respite from the media spotlight, and also offered us a glimpse of one of the Fifa World Cup stadia the Royals will be gracing later this week. Reading's clash with Lyon is apparently selling out and is expected to be the biggest match of the tournament. The country is waiting for this competition to start and clearly expecting big things from Steve Coppell's side. A short swim and some food ended a long, long opening day of Reading's pre-season tour.

As the team walked off the plane, the South Korean air stewardess smiled and shyly asked if a South Korean player played for us. Before the

Day Two: Wednesday, 11th July 2007

A good night's sleep was had by all and a big breakfast buffet awaited. The pastry basket remained relatively untouched though as most chose cereal, toast and fruit before their first foreign training session of the season. The coach filled at 10am and after a 30 minute drive the crazy driver steered the players' Peace Cup bus into an impressive sports complex.

'Welcome to Anyang City...Reading FC' was the message on the big screen and once again a mob of cameras flocked around the Royals stars, now joined by Seol; who stood in focus of every long lens throughout the two-hour workout. The pitch, surrounded by an athletics track was beautiful and the stadium was big. The weather though was a disaster. It is monsoon season in Seoul and from start to finish the Royals were put through their paces in torrential rain. The players were reassured by a helpful Peace Cup liaison team, that it is unusual to see the heavens open in such dramatic style, and that although more wet weather is forecast, they shouldn't expect such thunderous scenes every day.

Despite being soaked to the skin, everyone seemed to enjoy themselves in a few light training exercises – Adam Federici and Graham Stack were sliding from post to post trying to prevent Dave Kitson and Kevin Doyle finding the back of the net in the shooting drills, while Kalifa Cisse seemed completely comfortable on foreign soil with his new teammates.

Having dried out at the hotel and with some lunch inside them, the players were free to continue to get used to their new surroundings and Seol was a willing tour guide for many. An unmissable attraction below the hotel, is a shopping mall – the size of a small country! A multiplex cinema, designer clothes outlets, games arcades, noodle bars, and even an aquarium lie down an escalator from the hotel lobby and it would be a training exercise in itself if you wanted to walk through the whole place!

Day Three: Thursday, 12th July 2007

After Wednesday's powerful downpours Steve Coppell and his troops stepped off the air-conditioned coach into a wall of heat. With clouds a lot less menacing at 'Anyang City' and the temperature rising, the conditions couldn't have been more different; yesterday kit man Ron Grant was scurrying around for wet weather coats - today Dave Kitson was squirting sun tan lotion and Graham Stack looked a little uncomfortable in his all-black full-body goalkeeper's suit.

Every player kept themselves well hydrated with regular water breaks as the squad split for shooting and passing drills before a short game. It was difficult to tell how the boss was planning to line his side up for the first game against River Plate but it was fun trying to guess.

As Bolton were opening the Peace Cup with a 1-1 draw against Korean outfit Seongnam (in front of more than 40,000 people), James Henry and Alex Pearce travelled to a local 'SOS Village' on the outskirts of Seoul. Traffic seems to be a problem in Seoul and driving cars an even bigger one, but the two young Royals stars slept through most of the mayhem before arriving at their destination. As a favour to the British Council, Henry and Pearce gave a set of orphaned children a quick training session, which they loved. They especially enjoyed watching Henry do some ball-juggling tricks out in their playground. More traffic on the way back, but it was definitely a well worthwhile afternoon.

Day Four: Friday, 13th July 2007

The time had arrived for the Peace Cup to truly begin. It was Reading's turn to take centre stage. Little more than a year ago, only the most obsessive of the local Korean spectators who took to their seats in the Suwon Stadium would have recognised the blue and white hoops of Reading FC. Since the signing of Seol, it has all changed and although the right winger wasn't fit to start, the home support were only interested in cheering on one team – The Royals.

When the Reading players came out to warm up before kick off, rumble sticks, whistles and rattles echoed around the magnificent former Fifa World Cup venue, Steve Coppell and Dave Kitson's names were heard being chanted, a Reading FC banner was on show behind the Royals' goalmouth and even a flare was lit in the crowd to show their support. Team line-ups were introduced; each Reading photo was greeted with a hearty cheer. Kevin Doyle is a big star here; his goals last season seem to have made him a household name all over the world.

The South Americans dominated and controlled the pace of the game, keeping possession masterfully and choosing the right moment to attack dangerously. They kept shooting at Adam Federici's goal with a number of well-struck efforts testing the Australian keeper. And after the crossbar had been rattled and the left post hit, River Plate found the first goal with a beautifully curled free kick.

After the interval, the contest became much more even, with Michael Duberry and Kevin Doyle

close with headers but it stayed at 1-0 and the Royals were faced with a very a tough task if they were to top the group and qualify for the final.

Reading 0 – River Plate 1 (Abelairas) Friday, 13th July 2007

The Peace Cup – Group B, Suwon Stadium
Referee: Mr Choi Myung Yong

LINE-UPS: Reading (4-4-2):

Gk Federici
Rb Halls (Cisse)
Lb Shorey
cb Ingimarsson (Duberry)
cb Bikey
cm Gunnarsson
cm Harper
rm Oster (Hunt)
lm Robson-Kanu (Henry)
str Doyle
str Kitson

Subs not used: Stack, Murty, Golbourne, Pearce, Bennett, Cox, Long.

Yellow cards: Oster, Ingimarsson, Harper.

River Plate (4-4-2):

Gk Ojeda
rb Ferrari
lb Villagra
cb Tuzzio
cb Gerlo
cm Ponzio
cm Fernandez
rm Belluschi (Lima)
lm Abelairas
str Rosales (Falcao)
str Ruben

Subs not used: Leyenda, Bogado, Martinez, Lusenhoff, Burzac, Ahumada, Buonanotte, Cardozo, Etchemaite.

Yellow cards: Fernandez

Day Five: Saturday, 14th July 2007

Tired limbs were allowed a rest this morning as a light warm-down training session was scheduled for mid-afternoon. Some chose to participate in a short gym session with Jon Fearn late in the morning too.

One of the main complaints from players in previous tours has been the quality of Swedish television and South Korean TV is not much better. For that reason, John Oster and Graham Stack amongst others tested their skills with remote control cars in the hotel corridors before dinner. Some had media interviews to conduct.

After speaking to Sky Sports News and The Daily Mail after the defeat to River Plate, Nicky Shorey spoke to Gabby Logan on BBC Radio Five Live, Kevin Doyle did an interview with Jonathan Wall on the same station, Seol Ki-Hyeon did a piece with Korean TV station NBC and Steve Coppell spoke at length for a feature with Arena magazine. Adam Federici's piece with Talksport was postponed because the players' training session overran. Nicky Shorey temporarily lost the media hotline phone that was given to him but he soon found it again on the team bus.

Having moaned about the quality of the TV here, an English-speaking news channel did handily inform the players of a nearby typhoon; winds of over 200km per hour are hitting Japan at the moment. Shimizu S-Pulse, our opponents on Thursday, will be pleased they have left their homeland to come to Korea for this tournament!

Day Six: Sunday, 15th July 2007

No weekend rest for the Royals. A training session in the morning was followed by a second for some in the afternoon, while others tried to recharge their batteries with some afternoon sleep after lunch. A number of Royals stars including Dave Kitson, Seol Ki-Hyeon, John Oster, Brynjar Gunnarsson and Ivar Ingimarsson were mobbed by an estimated crowd of 500 people in the massive mall underneath our hotel in the afternoon as a public signing session raised more Royals eyebrows as their popularity in such a far flung location continued to amaze everyone. Meanwhile, the Club's Head of Communications, Andy West, was the Royals' representative at an international seminar organised by the Peace Cup committee for Korean clubs and the Far Eastern football industry in general. Others speaking at the seminar were from Bolton, Lyon and Real Madrid and 120 people crammed into the Olympic convention centre for the three-hour talk.

Steve Coppell and Jon Fearn opted for a less formal afternoon activity and in the searing heat chose to take in some baseball. The LG Twins were taking on the Kia Tigers and a 20,000 strong crowd went wild every time anything exciting happened. The rumble sticks were out again and this time, home and away supporters had a man with a microphone leading them all in chants as well as their own personal set of cheerleaders. Understanding the rules of baseball via a very complicated Korean scoreboard was not easy, but apparently the score was 3-1 in the seventh when they called it a day to come back for some food.

A few others from the travelling party wandered into the main Seoul '88 Olympic stadium. Although its size is still breathtaking, it is a little neglected and somewhat derelict now. The sky-high Olympic torch was unlit, the track unused and the stands totally empty - so it was difficult to visualise the excitement this city must have experienced when Ben Johnson famously romped home [illegally] in the 100m almost 20 years ago.

Day Seven: Monday, 16th July 2007

Fans were understandably disappointed to see the unfit Seol's name omitted from Steve Coppell's squad once more, but it was the man offered his midfield position against tonight's French opponents who grabbed the Group B headlines. Simon Cox did his very best to try to confuse a few South Korean journalists in tonight's post-match press conference by using the term 'bouncebackability' and I fear the emphasis of the word might have been a little lost in translation. But the Royals did 'bounce back' in serious style. Tonight's showing was much more impressive than the one that saw us beaten by River Plate three days ago and more importantly a win was earned and thoroughly deserved as Steve Coppell's side threw this Peace Cup group wide open.

Lyon won the Ligue 1 title for a sixth successive season last summer and despite the departure of Gerard Houllier and a slight change in personnel since that triumph, the French giants – one of the G14 clubs in Europe – were more than matched at the World Cup Stadium in Seoul tonight.

Cox, starting on the right side of midfield, scored the only goal of a thoroughly entertaining game. He burst into the box seeing Shane Long make progress down the Royals' right and showed good composure to slot home the Irish striker's pull back and notch Reading's first goal of the pre-season campaign. It was open, free-flowing, attractive and exciting football from both sides from the first to the final whistle. Kevin Doyle should have opened his account on two or three occasions in the first half; his best chance came from the spot, but after winning the penalty his 12-yarder was saved and Long tripped to scuff the follow up effort into the keeper's arms. Kalifa Cissé was a commanding figure in midfield alongside Harper (who had to be replaced after an aerial clash meant he needed a deep wound to his head stapled), while Scott Golbourne showed maturity beyond his years to make an exceptional contribution at left back in Nicky Shorey's absence.

Stephen Hunt looked lively throughout and both Andre Bikey and Michael Duberry looked at home without last season's player of the season at centre back alongside them; the ever present Ivar Ingimarsson enjoying a very rare rest. Graham Stack was called upon to tip a fantastic strike over his crossbar in the dying stages, but as a attacking outfit the likes of Milan Baros and Sydney Govou were competently shackled.

The boss has indicated that reaching the tournament's final is not the main objective and this competition is purely about preparing his players for the season ahead. In a similar way to last season's unstoppable surge towards a European place, Steve Coppell might have to work hard to slow the Royals progress in the Peace Cup too. A win against S-Pulse on Thursday combined with a lesser win for Lyon against the Argentinians would be enough to see Reading take an unlikely place in the final on Sunday. The Royals' stay may be yet be prolonged thanks to a stunning win against some of the best players in Europe. Stay tuned!

Reading 1 (Cox) – Lyon 0

Monday, 16th July 2007

The Peace Cup – Group B
The Seoul World Cup Stadium
Referee: Mr Kim Eui Soo

LINE-UPS: Reading (4-4-2):

- Gk Stack
- Rb Murty
- Lb Golbourne
- cb Duberry
- cb Bikey
- cm Cisse (Oster)
- cm Harper (Gunnarsson)
- rm Cox (Halls)
- lm Hunt
- str Doyle
- str Long

Subs not used: Federici, Shorey, Ingimarsson, Pearce, Bennett, Henry, Robson-Kanu, Kitson.

Yellow cards: Cisse, Golbourne.

LINE-UPS: Lyon (4-4-2):

- Gk Vercoutre
- rb Reveillere
- lb Belhadj
- cb Muller
- cb Cris (Paillot)
- cm Kallstrom
- cm Santos (Diarra)
- rm Bodmer (Govou)
- lm Mounier (Ben Arfa)
- str Baros (Benzema)
- str Keite (Loic)

Subs not used: Coupet, Hartock, Clerc, Grosso, Toulalan.

Yellow cards: Reveillere, Santos, Benzema.

Day Eight: Tuesday, 17th July 2007

Unlike the lay-in the players were given after the River Plate defeat, the coaching staff scheduled an early trip to the training ground for everyone this morning for a light warm down session. James Harper played a full part, without so much as a bandage around his wounded head, but with staples still secure and a plaster covering the injury. Seol took to the field with a strapped foot, but didn't join in any shooting drills which suggests he might struggle to feature in the competition. It would be disappointing for the South Korean fans who'd love to sample the atmosphere when Seol Ki-Hyeon is making his mazy runs in front of such staunch support. They scream when his face is put up on the big screen, so we can only imagine how high-pitched the reaction would be when our winger weaves past a petrified left back with the ball at his feet. But there is nothing Seol, nor Steve Coppell can do to speed the process up! We'll have to wait and hope.

A young team of local Korean children had clearly heard of Reading's presence in 'Anyang City' and stood watching the Royals arrive at training in awe. Players and coaches were all pleased to see the young admirers and Kevin Dillon beckoned over the wide-eyed boys to sit in a line along the touchline. If that hadn't already made their day, goalkeeping coach Sal Bibbo ensured one young keeper would enjoy an extra special morning, when he gave the budding Korean stopper a quick coaching session. They were thrilled - twenty new Royals fans for life had been effortlessly recruited.

A go-karting trip was organised for the afternoon and most of the playing staff took to the tracks to do battle. The youthful reactions behind the wheel of Shane Long saw the Irishman take the chequered flag, with John Halls'

strong challenge seen off by the Royals striker. Meanwhile, Ivar Ingimarsson, Brynjar Gunnarsson, Alan Bennett and others took time out to visit the famous Palace in Seoul. All returned for some food, and an early night, although some squeezed in a trip to see the new 'Transformers' film at an English-speaking cinema. Another early training session lies in wait for the Royals as they attempt to emulate Bolton's achievement (in getting to the final) and set up an all-Premiership meeting between the two teams on Saturday.

Day Nine: Wednesday, 18th July 2007

Another hot and humid morning saw the full squad train and work hard. After the last timetabled 10 o'clock leave, the coach didn't return to the hotel until after 2pm. Lunch and some free time in the afternoon for some; although Seoul is a built up westernised capital city, it is difficult to find things to do. It is so vast that most of the travelling party are still unsure if it has a centre or if the entire city is splayed in a very similar mould to the industrial part the hotel is based in. Most attractions seem to be a taxi ride away, and with traffic at a standstill throughout the daylight hours, not much can be achieved such short spells of free time. Plus, after hours of training in the morning and some still not fully adjusted to the time differences, a lot of the players just choose to rest in their rooms when they can.

Eight players were not allowed such luxuries. Graeme Murty, James Harper, Stephen Hunt, Simon Cox, John Halls, Scott Golbourne, Shane Long and Kevin Doyle were led into the shopping mall for the second of two signing stints set up by the Peace Cup officials. It was mayhem! More than 400 Korean fans could barely contain their excitement as gasps of amazement greeted the players on arrival. There is no doubt that Royalsmania has definitely hit the Far East.

It lasted an hour, but could have gone on for longer. Names were scrawled on Peace Cup autograph paper, home shirts that been brought along, bags, baseball caps and other items that were to hand. The long queue became steadily shorter as each player was politely asked to pose for a picture by every awe-struck fan that approached them, and at 4pm the eight players stood up and bowed in Korean style. They were followed back through the mall until security guards prevented the fans from following them up the escalator to the hotel's lobby. One man was not to be deterred though – he raced at full speed up the 'downward' escalator to keep up with the upwardly mobile James Harper while the Royals midfielder penned his name on another piece of paper.

Meanwhile, Seol Ki-Hyeon and some representatives from the Club went to the Korean FA headquarters to welcome the signing of three young Academy players recruited from Korea. It seems that the links with the Far East stretch further and deeper with every day.

Day Ten: Thursday, 19th July 2007

Escaping the endless drizzle of Seoul, the squad arrived at Goyang Stadium just before 7pm to begin a very humid pre-match walk around the pitch. The players were about to play a crucial Peace Cup group decider and it would be like doing battle within a low-lying cloud. You couldn't help but feel the conditions would test the European side more than their Japanese opponents. The complicated permutations which would see the Royals' stay in South Korea last a little longer basically boiled down to Reading needing a win, Lyon beating River Plate, and the Royals needing to better the French champions' scoreline. Bizarrely, in such foreign surroundings, Bolton await!

Another excellent advert for football richly rewarded the thousands that had turned out for the Royals versus Shimizu S-Pulse. The tempo was high from the start, the style was attractive and the game was another open, easy on the eye affair with chances at either end. Goalless at half time, Lyon led and it was suddenly within Reading's own grasp. Seol was on and producing all the tricks for his adoring public, and when substitute Brynjar Gunnarsson rose to power Dave Kitson's cross home, the belief that a place in the final was possible was strong. Reading pushed for an all-important second. Ivar Ingimarsson could have had a hat-trick - sending one header over, pushing one against the inside of the post and seeing a late stab somehow saved by the Japanese keeper.

In injury time James Harper broke the offside trap to sprint down the right wing and suggest a fairytale finale could be on the cards. He spotted Shane Long in open space and squared it perfectly for the Irish youngster, who calmly connected with a placed sidefoot. But Shimizu's goalkeeper was determined to spoil the Royals party and clung on low to his right and the final whistle followed. Reading had not done enough and Lyon actually scored a late third to oust ten-man River Plate and cement their place in Saturday's final.

To end on a win and to add a little drama to the Peace Cup competition, Steve Coppell's men were rightly pleased with their contribution. The boss has maintained throughout that the intentions on this trip were to prepare against quality opposition, and not to lift the silverware at the end of the tournament. But there is still a tinge of disappointment amongst the players – knowing that a place in the final was so close and that eighth-placed Reading could be exacting some revenge on seventh-placed Bolton in a couple of days time.

The tour though has been a success. Some of the journalists out here travelled to the final game on the South Korean tube system. On hi-tech screens positioned in every underground carriage, they were able to watch highlights from the Royals' previous

Reading 1 (Gunnarsson) – Shimizu S-Pulse 0
Thursday, 19th July 2007

**The Peace Cup – Group B, Goyang Stadium
Referee: Mr Kim Eui Soo**

LINE-UPS: Reading (4-4-2):

Gk Federici (Stack)
Rb Murty (Pearce)
Lb Shorey
cb Ingimarsson
cb Bennett
cm Harper
cm Cisse (Gunnarsson)
rm Oster (Seol)
lm Hunt (Robson-Kanu)
str Kitson
str Long

Subs not used: Halls, Golbourne, Bikey, Duberry, Henry, Cox, Doyle.

Yellow cards: Kitson, Robson-Kanu, Shorey.

LINE-UPS: Shimizu S-Pulse (4-4-2):

Gk Nishibe
rb Ichikawa
lb Kodama
cb Washita
cb Takagi
cm Ito
cm Fernando
rm Hyodo (Sugiyama)
lm Fujimoto
str Okazaki
str Yajima (Nishizawa)

Subs not used: Kakegawa, Hiramatsu, Takaki, Edamura, Hara, Hiraoka, Aoyama, Hiroi, Anderson.

Peace Cup encounters. How far this little Club have come! It speaks volumes for Reading's Premiership profile and popularity throughout the world. Reading have made their mark since arriving in south-east Asia and will take away fond memories of their South Korean adventure!

Player Profiles

ADAM FEDERICI

Position: Goalkeeper

Squad number: 32

Date of birth: 31st January 1985

Place of Birth: Nowra, Australia

Height: 6'2"

Signed: 20th September 2005

Fee: Free transfer

Previous clubs: Bristol City (on loan)

RFC Appearances: 4(+2)

RFC Goals: 0

MARCUS HAHNEMANN

Position: Goalkeeper

Squad number: 1

Date of birth: 15th June 1972

Place of Birth: Seattle, United States of America

Height: 6'3"

Signed: 8th August 2002

Fee: Free transfer

Previous clubs: Seattle Sounders, Colorado Rapids, Fulham, Rochdale (on loan)

RFC Appearances: 229(+1)

RFC Goals: 0

GRAHAM STACK

Position: Goalkeeper

Squad number: 21

Date of birth: 26th September 1981

Place of Birth: Hampstead, England

Height: 6'2"

Signed: 30th December 2005

Fee: Free transfer

Previous clubs: Arsenal, Beveren (on loan), Millwall

RFC Appearances: 10

RFC Goals: 0

NICKY SHOREY

Position: Left back

Squad number: 3

Date of birth: 19th February 1981

Place of Birth: Romford, England

Height: 5'10"

Signed: 9th February 2001

Fee: £25,000

Previous clubs: Leyton Orient

RFC Appearances: 258

RFC Goals: 10

ULISES DE LA CRUZ

Position: Full back

Squad number: 23

Date of birth: 8th February 1974

Place of Birth: Piquiucho, Ecuador

Height: 5'9"

Signed: 25th August 2006

Fee: Free transfer

Previous clubs: Deportivo Quito, Hibernian, Aston Villa

RFC Appearances: 15

RFC Goals: 1

IBRAHIMA SONKO

Position: Centre back

Squad number: 5

Date of birth: 22nd January 1981

Place of Birth: Bignola, Senegal

Height: 6'3"

Signed: 2nd July 2004

Fee: Free transfer

Previous clubs: Grenoble, Brentford

RFC Appearances: 113(+4)

RFC Goals: 5

IVAR INGIMARSSON

Position: Centre back

Squad number: 16

Date of birth: 20th August 1977

Place of Birth: Reykjavik, Iceland

Height: 6'0"

Signed: 23rd October 2003

Fee: £100,000

Previous clubs: Valur ÍBV, Torquay United (on loan), Brentford, Wolverhampton Wanderers, Brighton (on loan)

RFC Appearances: 169(+2)

RFC Goals: 9

ANDRE BIKEY

Position: Centre back

Squad number: 22

Date of birth: 8th January 1985

Place of Birth: Douala, Cameroon

Height: 6'0"

Signed: 1st August 2006

Fee: £1,000,000

Previous clubs: Espanyol, Marco de Canaveses, Paços de Ferreira, Desportivo das Aves, Shinnik Yaroslavl, Lokomotiv Moscow

RFC Appearances: 13(+8)

RFC Goals: 1

MICHAEL DUBERRY

Position: Centre back

Squad number: 29

Date of birth: 14th October 1975

Place of Birth: Enfield, England

Height: 6'1"

Signed: 31st January 2007

Fee: £800,000

Previous clubs: Chelsea, Bournemouth (loan), Leeds, Stoke

RFC Appearances: 8

RFC Goals: 0

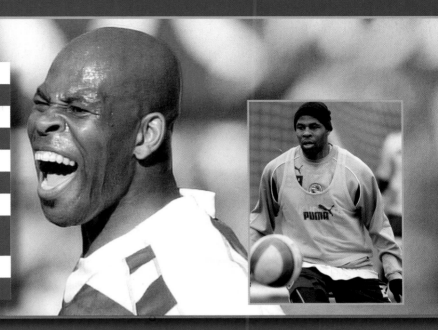

SAM SODJE

Position: Centre back

Squad number: 18

Date of birth: 29th May 1979

Place of Birth: Greenwich, England

Height: 6'0"

Signed: 14th July 2006

Fee: £350,000

Previous clubs: Stevenage Borough, Margate, Brentford

RFC Appearances: 4(+3)

RFC Goals: 1

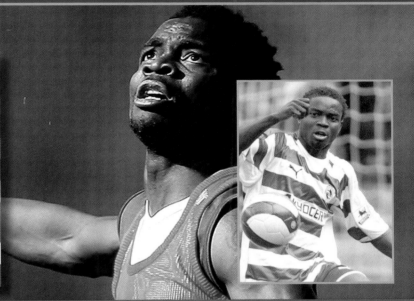

JOHN HALLS

Position: Right back / centre back

Squad number: 14

Date of birth: 14th February 1982

Place of Birth: Islington, London

Height: 6'0"

Signed: 19th January 2006

Fee: £250,000

Previous clubs: Arsenal, Colchester United (loan), Beveren (loan), Stoke City

RFC Appearances: 5

RFC Goals: 1

JAMES HARPER

Position: Centre midfield

Squad number: 15

Date of birth: 9th November 1980

Place of Birth: Chelmsford, England

Height: 5'10"

Signed: 28th February 2001

Fee: Undisclosed

Previous clubs: Arsenal, Cardiff City (on loan)

RFC Appearances: 238(+25)

RFC Goals: 19

BRYNJAR GUNNARSSON

Position: Centre midfield

Squad number: 6

Date of birth: 16th October 1975

Place of Birth: Reykjavik, Iceland

Height: 6'1"

Signed: 22nd July 2005

Fee: Undisclosed

Previous clubs: KR Reykjavík, Vålerenga, Moss (on loan), Örgryte IS, Stoke City, Nottingham Forest, Watford

RFC Appearances: 37(+24)

RFC Goals: 8

KALIFA CISSE

Position: Centre midfield

Squad number: 4

Date of birth: 1st September 1984

Place of Birth: Dreux, France

Height: 6'2"

Signed: 16th May 2007

Fee: £650,000

Previous clubs: Toulouse, Estoril, Boavista

RFC Appearances: 0

RFC Goals: 0

GLEN LITTLE

Position: Right midfield

Squad number: 7

Date of birth: 15th October 1975

Place of Birth: Wimbledon, England

Height: 6'3"

Signed: 30th June 2004

Fee: Free transfer

Previous clubs: Crystal Palace, Glentoran, Burnley, Bolton Wanderers (on loan)

RFC Appearances: 94(+18)

RFC Goals: 6

JOHN OSTER

Position: Right midfield

Squad number: 11

Date of birth: 8th December 1978

Place of Birth: Boston, England

Height: 5'9"

Signed: 2nd August 2005

Fee: Free transfer

Previous clubs: Grimsby Town, Everton, Sunderland, Barnsley (on loan), Leeds United (on loan), Burnley

RFC Appearances: 31(+41)

RFC Goals: 3

BOBBY CONVEY

Position: Left midfield

Squad number: 17

Date of birth: 27th May 1983

Place of Birth: Philadelphia, USA

Height: 5'8"

Signed: 23rd July 2004

Fee: Undisclosed

Previous clubs: DC United

RFC Appearances: 63(+16)

RFC Goals: 7

STEPHEN HUNT

Position:	Left midfield
Squad number:	10
Date of birth:	1st August 1980
Place of Birth:	County Laois, Republic of Ireland
Height:	5'9"
Signed:	29th June 2005
Fee:	Free transfer
Previous clubs:	Crystal Palace, Brentford
RFC Appearances:	41(+43)
RFC Goals:	7

SEOL KI-HYEON

Position:	Right midfield / Striker
Squad number:	19
Date of birth:	8th January 1979
Place of Birth:	Jeongseon, South Korea
Height:	6'0"
Signed:	11th July 2006
Fee:	£1,500,000
Previous clubs:	Antwerp, Anderlecht, Wolverhampton Wanderers.
RFC Appearances:	26(+5)
RFC Goals:	4

KEVIN DOYLE

Position:	Striker
Squad number:	9
Date of birth:	18th September 1983
Place of Birth:	Adamstown, Republic of Ireland
Height:	5'11"
Signed:	7th June 2005
Fee:	Undisclosed
Previous clubs:	St Patrick's Athletic, Cork City
RFC Appearances:	72(+13)
RFC Goals:	33

LEROY LITA

Position: Striker
Squad number: 8
Date of birth: 28th December 1984
Place of Birth: Kinshasa, Democratic Republic of Congo
Height: 5'7"
Signed: 14th July 2005
Fee: £1,000,000
Previous clubs: Bristol City
RFC Appearances: 52(+19)
RFC Goals: 29

DAVE KITSON

Position: Striker
Squad number: 12
Date of birth: 21st January 1980
Place of Birth: Hitchin, England
Height: 6'3"
Signed: 26th December 2003
Fee: £150,000
Previous clubs: Arlesey Town, Cambridge United
RFC Appearances: 92(+19)
RFC Goals: 51

SHANE LONG

Position: Striker
Squad number: 12
Date of birth: 22nd January 1987
Place of Birth: Gortnahoe, Republic of Ireland
Height: 5'10"
Signed: 7th June 2005
Fee: Nominal
Previous clubs: Cork City
RFC Appearances: 17(+22)
RFC Goals: 8

Stay tuned to readingfc.co.uk for all the latest on the Royals!

This summer the Club's official website readingfc.co.uk became even better than ever!

The Club launched their new-look official website in the close season, and the redesign takes the site forward and most importantly makes it easier for you to find everything you need to know about the Royals.

readingfc.co.uk is your first port of call for all things related to the Royals, from the first team to the Academy and all our Club activities in between.

You don't have to login or register for any part of readingfc.co.uk now. You can still register if you want to receive our official email newsletter and news direct to your inbox, but no passwords are needed now to look at any part of the site.

Also, it is much easier to find whatever you are looking for with one simple click from the homepage.

NEWS Besides the Latest News section, which predominantly keeps you up to date with all the first team news, we now have nine additional news sections which offer you the latest ticket news, information on our Community exploits, as well as keeping you informed from the Academy, Megastore, Commercial department and more.

VIDEO Our online TV station Reading World is bigger and better. The quality of our videos has been improved and we have all the behind the scenes access to give you pre and post-match interviews unseen anywhere else. Highlights from every first team and reserve game are available to watch any time day or night, and you won't miss a thing with our online TV station. Plus now, the vast majority of Reading World videos will now come with a short preview clip that anybody can watch... **absolutely free!**

BLOGS One of our new sections will feature blogs from the very heart of Reading FC. With regular columnists, you'll be able to get a behind the scenes insight, read expert opinions and share in other fans' verdicts.

PHOTOS You can see the popular picture specials in a great new gallery tool, which gives you much bigger pictures, quicker and easier.

ON THE MOVE Top stories are now available on your mobile phone with our mobile internet site. You can also get breaking stories sent instantly by text message with our official SMS. See the Mobile Services page online for more details.

Stephen Hunt

Steve Coppell
A Tribute

We think Steve Coppell's great. And we're not alone – here are the views on our boss of a selection of players pundits and managers...

Alan Hansen: "When you talk about honesty and integrity in this game, Steve Coppell is the man! The way his team embraced the Premiership was a breath of fresh air."

Richard Keys: "Steve Coppell is a big reason why Reading have succeeded where so many have failed. He's a very clever and thoughtful manager who has played the 'we're very naïve' card to great effect."

Sir Alex Ferguson: "He doesn't get too emotional. He's a calm, intelligent lad. When we played Palace in the 1990 final, he had a really feisty team, all warriors. It was an example of how he's able to bond together good pros with a good, winning attitude."

Mark Bright: "Steve Coppell was the best manager I ever played for. I say that without any disrespect to any of the others I worked with, but Steve was the best for me. I was in Leicester's reserves when he took me to Crystal Palace, and while he didn't give me any more ability, he built my confidence and the combination with Ian Wright. He treats players in the right way. He demands a lot, but he helps you as a person and in your life. He is also totally different away from the media spotlight. He's a funny person with a dry sense of humour which doesn't always come across on the camera."

Ian Wright: "Steve Coppell means the world to me, he's a father figure. I respect him immensely and feel humbled in his presence. Everyone needs a chance in life and he gave me a chance when I was working on a building site. He has been a major influence on my life and I love him. The best thing about Steve is that he only demands from his players what he knows they can give, and then he shows faith in them."

John Motson: "I knew Steve as a young player at Manchester United in the 1970s, and there is no question that he was a keen student of the game even then. He has used the know-how he earned from managing in the lower leagues to great effect with Reading. His great quality is managing to keep his feet on the ground at all times - he never gets carried away! There were some big compliments paid to him by people in our office after the 1-0 win at Fulham. How often do you hear a manager face the cameras and admit an opponent shouldn't have been sent off? That honest reaction really got the tongues wagging, because we're so used to managers berating officials for decisions that have gone against them. Sympathising with Ian Pearce and Fulham showed great maturity."

Alan Smith: "Steve brings a sense of perspective. When Reading do suffer a couple of defeats, Steve will say the right things to calm them down before going again. There is a wealth of experience to call upon if the players need to and it seems they feel safe knowing much of their destiny lies in his hands."

Arsene Wenger: "Steve Coppell 's team in are a position where nobody expected and he has a team who do not play negatively - they have a positive attitude everywhere they go."

Tommy Docherty (former Manchester United manager): "Steve was one of the best players I ever had the privilege of working with. I loved having him in my team because, as a manager, he gave you peace of mind. I never had to worry about him having a bad game, because he just didn't have them."

Gareth Southgate: "Steve has always been a top manager and he has worked wonders with Reading. Their success is down to his leadership and I have the utmost respect for him. I still think about the methods he adopted at Palace and the type of players he introduced to the club."

Steve Bruce: "Steve has done a fantastic job over the years and whatever club he's been at, he's been successful. People talk about good English managers and I think Steve Coppell is right up there with any of them."

Jose Mourinho: "He is doing brilliant work and I applaud it. His side do not try just to get a draw. They are well organised and play at high intensity."

Kerry Mayo (Brighton & Hove Albion): "Steve Coppell is certainly the most influential manager I have had to date, regarding my own game. I played every game when he was here. I had so much confidence because he let me go out there and play my own game. I feel Reading will be challenging for a UEFA spot this season."

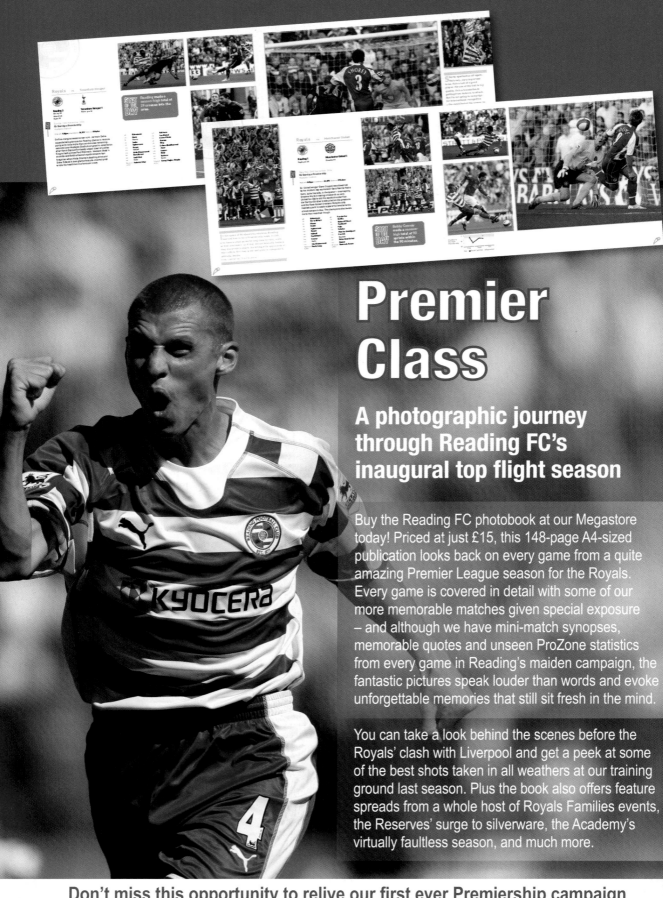

Premier Class

A photographic journey through Reading FC's inaugural top flight season

Buy the Reading FC photobook at our Megastore today! Priced at just £15, this 148-page A4-sized publication looks back on every game from a quite amazing Premier League season for the Royals. Every game is covered in detail with some of our more memorable matches given special exposure – and although we have mini-match synopses, memorable quotes and unseen ProZone statistics from every game in Reading's maiden campaign, the fantastic pictures speak louder than words and evoke unforgettable memories that still sit fresh in the mind.

You can take a look behind the scenes before the Royals' clash with Liverpool and get a peek at some of the best shots taken in all weathers at our training ground last season. Plus the book also offers feature spreads from a whole host of Royals Families events, the Reserves' surge to silverware, the Academy's virtually faultless season, and much more.

Don't miss this opportunity to relive our first ever Premiership campaign in full technicolour with some of the best pictures from the photographers who followed the Royals throughout.

Seol Ki-Hyeon

Sharp Shooter

Leroy stars in epic effort from England

When striker Leroy Lita was interviewed by the Royals' official matchday programme before an infamous Premiership encounter with Chelsea last season, he thought he'd been totally forgotten by the England under-21 set-up – to the extent that the £1m frontman wasn't even sure if, as he approached his 22nd birthday, he was still eligible. Eight months later, Lita seemed to be single-handedly steering the side to a European under-21 Championship Final until the Royals sharp-shooter was forced to witness a calamitous end to the campaign from the confines of the bench in Heerenveen.

Stuart Pearce's appointment breathed new life into Lita's under-21 involvement – first being recalled for the first competitive match to be held at the new Wembley Stadium in mid-March. Despite leading the line in that 3-3 thriller and then scoring from the bench in England's final build-up match before the tournament - a 5-0 drubbing of Slovakia at Carrow Road - he was left out of the starting line-up for the first game of the competition; a goalless draw with the Czech Republic in Arnhem. Unfortunately, despite making a very positive impact after his 64th minute emergence from the bench, Lita's name was associated mostly with a last gasp penalty miss that denied England three valuable points.

Lesser characters would have leapt into the shadows of the 21-man squad but Lita has praiseworthy and deserved faith in his own ability. "I never doubt myself. If I make a mistake, I'll hold my hands up, I'll never hide and I'll make sure I'm there for the next one," the Royals striker reassured his doubters. "The only way you can put it right is by getting up and doing it again. If you want to be successful you've got to be prepared for the downfalls. I'm prepared to take that on board. All the great players have gone through bad patches or made mistakes and as long as you don't get yourself down then you'll be able to bounce back." And he did. Pearce had confidence in the Royals strike sensation and picked him to start in a crucial clash with one of the tournament favourites only three days later. And, in the same city that had seen him drag his spotkick wide of the woodwork, Lita notched the second of two as Italy found themselves 2-0 down within the first 26 minutes. "I love scoring goals and the celebrations today showed that, I hope I can celebrate more goals like that out here," Lita beamed. "I got a few abusive messages after missing the penalty in the last game, but I just ignored them and concentrated on doing my thing on the pitch."

The Italians fought back to clinch a point but Lita's attitude and impact was impressing everyone in Holland and those watching back at home. "I was disappointed for him when he missed that penalty in the first game, but the way he's bounced back has been tremendous," his club captain told the Royals' official website. "It would have been easy for him to go under and hide," Graeme Murty continued, "but he's not that kind of person. He always wants to show how good he is and he took it all in his stride. He's showed fantastic character and he's now getting his just desserts. Leroy is playing at the top of the game and always looks like scoring goals. For me, he's been the pick of England's strikers."

The Congo-born striker had to deal with a different challenge in the final group game. English players were taunted and subject to some volatile racial abuse from Serbian supporters during a 2-0 win in Nijmegen; a game in which Lita again found himself on the scoresheet after a 5th minute far post finish set up a crucial 2-0 victory. When asked about the reception some of the English players received from certain Serbian quarters of the De Goffert Stadion, Lita showed admirable restraint and maturity in his condemnation of the derision, saying "Justin [Hoyte] took a lot of stick and he is not very happy, but as I said to him we can't worry about things like that, you just move on. We are here playing in a tournament, everyone just

"Leroy is playing at the top of the game & always looks like scoring goals. For me, he's been the pick of England's strikers."

"If you want to be successful you've got to be prepared for the downfalls."

wants to enjoy themselves and there is no need for that. But we will forget about it, we are through and we will think about Wednesday's semi-final."

Lita and England were playing well and a meeting with their Dutch hosts held little fear for Pearce's men. The now irrepressible Lita struck a sweet left-footed volley to fire England into the lead before the break, before cannoning a free-kick against the woodwork soon after the interval. Holland were running out of time and ideas when Lita was taken off for Anton Ferdinand in the 87th minute. Two minutes later, Maceo Rigters took advantage of a hobbling Steven Taylor to hook a desperately late overhead kick past Scott Carson and under the crossbar to haul a bedraggled England side into the torture of extra time.

Somehow, they held on – despite losing Nedum Onuoha to injury and playing the 30 minutes with ten (and effectively nine considering the brave Taylor could barely stand) very tired men. England and penalties just don't mix but the Dutch have had their fair share of shootout disappointment in the past – as a result it took 32 attempts to separate the sides but Foppe de Haan's men ran out eventual 13-12 victors on penalties. So Lita's under-21 career came to an untimely end in a team huddle in the centre circle in the Abe Lenstra Stadion in Heerenveen – and all he could do was watch the man who had replaced him in the dying stages of normal time slice his 12-yarder onto the crossbar to deny the Royals striker a fitting finale to his under-21 involvement. But with the attitude and ability he had shown the world throughout the Championships, only a fool would bet against Leroy Lita lining up in a senior England side in the not too distant future!!

"The players can be extremely proud of themselves for what they've achieved and the whole country can be proud too," were Steve McClaren's words after the semi-final defeat. "That's one in the bank for the players out there tonight. The experience they will take away from tonight and the tournament will be invaluable. It's for the future and it can only make them better players. When they have to face situations like that again, they'll be able to take from what they have learned here."

MAKING HISTORY

3.43pm, Saturday 19th August 2006, and history is made when Dave Kitson pokes the ball over the line to score Reading's first ever goal in the top flight of English football!

Whatever happens over the remainder of his career, Kits will always command a special place in the Reading Football Club history books, and the striker said, "Looking back on it now, it's a big thing for me. At the time I was too caught up in the emotion of trying to win the game to really appreciate it, but it's something I'll always be able to look back on and bore people with!"

As well as marking a significant milestone in the history of the Club, the goal was also hugely important in the more immediate context of that afternoon's game. The Royals had fallen into an early deficit against Middlesbrough but Kits' strike sparked a dramatic recovery which culminated in a thrilling 3-2 victory.

Recalling the goal itself, Dave says, "When we went 2-0 down, at home on the opening day of the season, I was thinking that we were going to have a very tough season! I knew we needed to get a goal back as soon as possible.

"I remember the ball going over to Seol on the right wing, and he made some space for a cross which he can do so well. Then he drilled the ball across the six yard box and it hit me on my left knee.

"When it dropped inside the six yard box, I knew that I just need to get something on it. Mark Schwarzer was diving across and Chris Riggott had his hand on my shoulder, but I just managed to get my toe on the ball and that was all it needed!

"When the ball went in, my first thought was 'get the ball!' because I wanted to restart play as quickly as possible and continue to put them under pressure. I knew that if we got another goal, we would win the game. So I just ran into the net and grabbed the ball, and it was only when I was running back to the halfway line that it hit me – I had scored Reading's first goal in the Premiership! "But that emotion didn't last for long, because the main feeling was just wanting us to score another goal. We were pummeling them at that stage, and of course it didn't take long before Siddy scored again to make it 2-2."

However, Kits' delight was soon quashed when he suffered a serious knee injury in a poor challenge from Boro defender Chris Riggott, and the striker admits that the injury put a dampener on his post-match celebrations.

"When it dropped inside the six yard box, I knew that I just need to get something on it."

"To be honest, after the game I felt quite hollow. I had scored the first goal and we'd won the game, but I knew that I was going to be out for a long time. Everybody was asking me about the goal and the excitement of the victory, but for me the joy was washed away by the injury and I felt empty.

"It overshadowed everything and it's only now that I'm fully fit again that I can look back and think, yes, that's a really nice thing that I scored Reading's first Premiership goal. Nobody can ever take that away from me!"

HISTORY MAKERS

Other significant 'firsts' in our history.

21st February 1872 – Reading 0-0 Reading Grammar School
The very first game in Reading Football Club's history! The encounter at King's Meadow may have been a less than thrilling goalless draw, but we were underway!

6th March 1875 – England 2-2 Scotland
Edward Brownlow Haygarth becomes Reading's first England international, filling the right back role at The Oval. He was never selected for the national team again!

28th August 1920 – Newport County 0-1 Reading
Our first match in the Football League ends in triumph as Joe Bailey nets the only goal in south Wales. We were competing in Division Three South after being elected to step up from the Southern League.

1st May 1926 – Reading 7-1 Brentford
Our first promotion! Victory – and promotion to Division Two – was sealed thanks to four goals from Frank Richardson and a hat-trick from Hugh Davey in front of 17,432 spectators at Elm Park.

22nd August 1998 – Reading 3-0 Luton Town
Madejski Stadium opens its doors for the very first time! Tommy Burns' team marked the occasion with an excellent victory, and it took midfielder Grant Brebner less than ten minutes to net the historic first goal at the new home of the Royals!

Shane Long

Bienvenue Cissé!

Kalifa prepared to fill some big boots

The Royals' first season in the Premier League was a success! When most were predicting a relegation struggle, Steve Coppell's side strode defiantly to an 8th placed finish. One of the key elements behind the newcomers' immediate progress amongst the country's best was the unity and togetherness within the squad. Steve Sidwell's long-anticipated departure to Chelsea threatened to remove a driving force from Reading's engine room and leave a sizeable hole at the heart of the Royals midfield. But a series of scouting missions had identified the player all loyal Royals will be hoping can fill that void.

Chief Scout, Brian McDermott, was the first member of our coaching staff to watch Kalifa Cissé in action for Boavista, and instinctively he was attracted to the towering midfielder's ability. "We first started looking at him earlier in the year, when I got a DVD of Kalifa playing. Since

Kalifa is a 6'2" central midfielder who is also capable of playing at centre back. He signed a three-year contract with Reading on 16th May 2007.

then, I've been out to see him, and so have Nick [Hammond] and

The Royals paid just under €1,000,000, which is about £650,000, to Portuguese top flight side Boavista for Cissé's services.

Steve [Coppell]. He's obviously versatile because we've seen him play in midfield and at the back,

He made his full Reading debut in Reading's 1-0 preseason win against French champions Lyon. He was harshly booked for a high foot by referee Kim Eui Soo but looked comfortable alongside James Harper and then Brynjar Gunnarsson in central midfield.

he's strong and he's got nous."

It's clear that, amongst others who have now seen Kalifa parade his skills in the blue and white hoops, McDermott believes the Club have got themselves a summer bargain. "This deal might have been difficult if we had left it longer. We knew there were other clubs interested so we wanted it done quickly and quietly so nobody could jump in. His name didn't come out at all, which was good for us."

"He has real athletic ability and the technical attributes that should be well suited to the Premiership. Having spent time with him and his family in Portugal, we believe he will adapt quickly to life in England and his personality will fit very well with the current squad." **Nick Hammond, Director of Football.**

"To sign Kalifa so soon after the end of the season shows this Club's ambition to do well in the Premiership next year. I'd like to welcome this very highly regarded player to Reading, and I'm delighted we've secured his signature." **John Madejski, Chairman.**

And the graceful but powerful midfielder is already enjoying the start of his three-year stay at Madejski Stadium. "I love it here. The training ground looks good, the staff's training techniques are good and I even have some French players to talk to. There is a great ambiance here so I am very, very happy. To play in the Premier League is a dream I have been following for a long time and now it is a dream I can realise."

Cissé was given the Royals' no.4 shirt vacated by Steve Sidwell this summer.

"I was very pleased with what he did. With him being French, I was keen for him to start against a French team. I thought it would help make him comfortable because it can be a steep learning curve to integrate into the team. He had a good night's work." **Steve Coppell, Manager (after Kalifa Cissé's start for the Royals)**

The 22-year-old Frenchman missed just three of Boavista's games last season, the last coming after he had penned a deal at Madejski Stadium. He helped the Panthers reach 10th spot in the Portuguese Liga as well as the quarter-final of their domestic cup competition.

The towering midfielder was born on 1st September 1984 in Dreux, a town in north-west France.

"He looks like Vieira and runs like Vieira. He has the same way of running with his arms tucked in by his side. He looks to be a good signing and hopefully he can settle in quickly and show what he can do in the Premiership."
Graeme Murty, Captain.

In his first interview after signing the contract, Cisse mentioned that he had met Steve Coppell and already knew of the Royals boss. "I know the manager is famous and saw that he received some awards at the end of the season. I think we will work well together," he confidently told the Club's official online TV station. Time will tell, but it looks like Coppell might have beaten off early close season competition to make a shrewd addition to his well-balanced Royals squad.

"Everyone tells me that I am a very fast and aggressive player," remarked Cissé. They are qualities that Sidwell had in abundance. To expect the Frenchman to immediately match Sidwell's return - 30 goals from 186 appearances – is asking too much too soon. But early signs in preseason suggest he already has a synchronicity with James Harper and is comfortable playing Reading's attractive style of football.

Before spending two years with Boavista, Cissé had previously played for GD Estoril (currently in the Liga de Honra – the Portuguese equivalent of the Championship) and began as a youngster with Toulouse in his native France.

Cissé is yet to be capped by his country at senior level.

Kalifa made his first appearance in a Royals shirt as a 71st minute substitute for John Halls in Reading's Peace Cup opener against River Plate.

"He's our type of player. He's young, he's hungry, and he's desperate to do well. "He's a good age and he'll fit in with our players. It's a typically good signing of ours." **Brian McDermott, Chief Scout.**

Taking aim!

Kevin Doyle promising more goals to come

Two years ago, Kevin Doyle (a relatively anonymous 21-year-old striker playing for Cork City in the Eircom league in Ireland) signed a contract with Reading FC (an up-and-coming English football club playing in the top tier of the Football League but yet to realise their top flight ambitions in their 134-year long history). 18 months later an accomplished Irish international sat alongside Didier Drogba at the top of the Premier League's goalscoring charts as Doyle helped guide Steve Coppell's newcomers into an astonishing eight-placed finish. Press pundits are already diagnosing Reading's forthcoming demise as a symptom of the dreaded 'second season syndrome', but despite a daunting start to the season, the Royals star striker is confident his side can find a cure and succeed amongst the English elite for a second successive season.

"I'm not thinking about who we are playing or what the score in the game is - I'm just thinking 'I've got a penalty!'"

It's almost time to start a new season in the Barclays Premier League – and it couldn't be a much tougher opening for the Royals. What was your reaction when you saw that Sir Alex's side had been pitted against us on the opening weekend?

"It is obviously a very tough start. Ideally, you'd want a much easier beginning to the season, with a game you could expect to get something from. No-one will expect us to get anything out of Manchester United away. But we got a point against them at home last year and drew with them in the Cup at Old Trafford. We have to play them at some point and we know, after last season, that we are capable of getting something. This year, we will have been there before which will hopefully help. You never know we might just nick a surprising result with a bit of luck!"

And then Chelsea at home three days later! Last year we drew with Manchester United home and away, drew with Chelsea, earned more than we were rewarded with from our three games against Liverpool. This year, can we do the same or even go one better and beat the big four teams?

"I hope so. We're more experienced and hopefully we'll get a bit more luck when we need it this season. We were unlucky with Chelsea's deflected goal last season and a couple of times things just didn't go our way. We might not manage wins against these teams, but we'll certainly give it a go! When Manchester United came to us last year, we went ahead...and we nearly held on. Maybe this year we will. There is not going to be any pressure on us – all of the pressure will be on them!"

Kevin, you scored the opening goal in that game to give us the lead from the spot against United. Can you remember how it felt to see the ball squeeze past Edwin Van der Sar?

"It was just a great feeling. It was just sheer relief, more than happiness to be honest. Especially with penalties – it's just a release of pressure when you score, because there is always such a big build up. It must have been at least a minute, before I got to take that one. When I step up to take a penalty, I'm not thinking about who we are playing or what the score in the game is - I'm just thinking 'I've got a penalty!'. Then you see Van der Sar in front of you - he's pretty big and the goal looks very small. So it was very nice to see it go in."

If you get the chance, and a penalty comes along at Old Trafford on the opening Sunday afternoon – will you be first to the ball? And will you feel even more pressure, taking a spotkick in front of three times the number of people as 70,000 United fans watch on?

"It won't be any different I don't think. The crowd doesn't make too big a difference when you place the ball on the spot. It's not as noticeable when you are lining up to take a penalty. In fairness, if the crowd does make a difference it is definitely going to make a difference at Old Trafford. I'll be nervous...but nerves help!"

Reading fans knew all about your goalscoring pedigree well before the Premier League was given its first taste of Reading FC last season, but having scored 13 top flight goals, what will be your personal aims in 2007/8?

"To stay fit and get better! My only aim is to at least match but preferably go better than last season. It won't be easy. If I can get into double figures again it will be a great return and I'll be very happy if I can beat last season's total. That would be my target – I know it'll be very difficult but that's my aim. I always aim to improve and as a striker, to improve, you need to score more goals."

In Seol-Ki-Hyeon's absence during much of our preseason Peace Cup tour, your name on the teamsheet was the name that thrilled thousands of South Korean fans. You're now a big star within this Reading team – how are you coping with the new-found fame? Is more expected of you than when you first arrived at the Club?

"I think there is more expected of me this season, but that shows how well I did last season. So you have to deal with it. If I play well, that is something I have to get used to and it's up to me to do so as best I can. It's obviously a strange feeling seeing South Korean people shouting your name and flashing their cameras at you – but it's nice! To some extent, it's the same for all the players. We finished eighth last year and to ensure we get invitations to tournaments like the Peace Cup we have to keep doing well, this season and hopefully for many years to come.

You mentioned our eighth-placed finish last season - is it realistic to aim for a position as high as that again this year?

"I think to finish in the top half this season would be a great achievement. The second season and the warnings that come with that 'second season', suggest finishing in eighth, ninth or tenth would be brilliant. Even if we finished a couple of places below that, it would still turn out to be a fantastic season for us. That will be our aim. Obviously we want to beat what we did last season, but it's not possible to climb much higher without spending millions and millions of pounds. We're obviously not a club that is going to do that and we know that a repeat of last season would be another excellent campaign."

History tells us that the second season is always much tougher than the first in the Premier League. And Steve Coppell has talked about how we will be playing without last season's 'surprise element'. With people knowing a bit more about how you and Reading play, will that make beating teams much harder this season?

"I think it will. But in the same way that other teams will know more about us, we'll be a bit more prepared for them as well. This season we'll all be a lot more accustomed to the whole Premiership experience and it is up to us to not get carried away. We have to keep our feet on the ground and try to play more good football whenever we walk out onto the pitch. If we can do that, and if everyone stays at the top of their game, we should be fine again. We'll need a bit of luck too – injuries need to go our way. But hopefully, touch wood, we will be ok."

Season review DVD in stock now

Our 2006/7 official two-disc DVD is in the Megastore now.

Visit the Megastore to get your hands on a copy, or order now in the online store to have it posted out.

Featuring every game from the 6th December onwards, this double-disc set looks back on the finish to an amazing debut season in the top flight.

With our 6-0 win over West Ham, the 3-1 over Sheffield United, both great FA Cups with Manchester United and much, much more, it's a brilliant memento of a superb campaign.

Quiz Answers

THE SEASON:
August: Sam Sodje
September: Kevin Doyle
October: Marcus Hahnemann, Jonathan Hayes, Curtis Osano and Pierre Joseph-Dubois.
November: Hossam Ghaly
December: Kevin Doyle
January: Brynjar Gunnarsson
February: Everton
March: Brazil
April: Stephen Hunt
May: Tottenham Hotspur (a)

THE OPPOSITION:
1. Julio Arca
2. Pedro Mendes
3. Michael Essien, Anton Ferdinand, Joleon Lescott, Cesc Fabregas
4. Ousmane Dabo
5. Dirk Kuyt and Cristiano Ronaldo

INTERNATIONALS:
1. Doyle against San Marino (5-0) in November, and Long versus Bolivia (1-1) in May
2. 3-1 against Albania at Burnley's Turf Moor.
3. Ulises De La Cruz, for Ecuador
4. Alan Bennett
5. Seol Ki-Hyeon (for South Korea in a 2-0 defeat in Hanover)

SEASON'S END:
1. Michael Dobson led Walsall to the top of League Two
2. Jonathan Hayes (on loan at MK Dons) and Sam Sodje (on loan at West Bromwich Albion).
3. Kalifa Cissé
4. Aston Villa
5. Wayne Rooney, Cristiano Ronaldo, Cesc Fabregas, Aaron Lennon and Micah Richards

TRIVIA
1. Ibrahima Sonko (vs Aston Villa), Andre Bikey (vs Chelsea) and Sam Sodje (vs Manchester United)
2. Phil Jagielka (Sheffield United), Richard Dunne (Manchester City) and Joseph Yobo (Everton)
3. Peter Mate; he scored one goal in the 3-3 Carling Cup draw with Darlington before suffering a cruciate knee ligament injury
4. Graeme Murty, Ivar Ingimarsson and Brynjar Gunnarsson (against Darlington)
5. 30%

NAME THAT PLAYER
1. Leroy Lita
2. Adam Federici
3. Seol Ki-Hyeon
4. Ibrahima Sonko
5. Shane Long
6. James Harper

Reading Football Club's community team comprises eight full-time qualified coaches and 30 part-time staff who cover a wide region offering specialist football coaching to schools and clubs. The club also organises a large number of their own events, such as the ever-popular soccer schools which welcome hundreds of children during every school holiday. The club's aim is to take Reading FC into the local community as much as possible, but they are also expanding their horizons and looking overseas and during recent months the club has visited the USA, Germany, France, Ireland and Bermuda to undertake community coaching initiatives.

READING-BERMUDA CULTURAL LINK

Reading's recent rise to the Premiership has seen the club's profile spread to the international stage, and the community department has been proud to develop strong links on the island of Bermuda.

The club first came into contact with Bermuda through former Royals striker Shaun Goater, whose spell at the Madejski Stadium enabled the club to make contact and form a link with Pembroke Hamilton Club, a Premier League side in Bermuda.

In April 2007, community coaches Lee Herron and Ryan Williams made a week-long visit to the island, working alongside the Pembroke Hamilton coaches to run a soccer school for more than 130 local children, who were very excited by the opportunity to learn from representatives of an English Premier League team.

Mark Wade, director of coaching for Pembroke Hamilton, said, "The support of Reading Football Club was invaluable during our first football camp. All feedback from the parents and players has been very positive and everyone is asking about next year already. The players were able to experience a different type of coaching and enjoyed the exposure.

"Pembroke Hamilton coaches were able to talk with Lee and Ryan during a coaching seminar which gave us an insight into the coaching techniques geared toward preparing players for a professional career. Overall the camp and interaction was very rewarding for all concerned."

The trip was extremely successful and further visits are planned. And to continue the good relationship between the two parties, this summer Pembroke Hamilton's under-14 squad visited Reading to play a number of British sides, and the club has also set up a cultural link between Hillside School in Reading and Victor Scott School in Bermuda, allowing the children to regularly interact and provide an insight into each other's lives and cultures.

ROYALS ROADSHOW

Around 2,000 children at 20 different schools in Berkshire have attended the Royals Roadshow in the last two years.

In association with the club's community sponsors ADT, the theme of the Roadshow was 'Arson: Strike It Out', combining football fun and educational messages about fire safety. Each visit lasted two hours and contained a football coaching session from the club's Football in the Community staff, a fire safety presentation from ADT and the Berkshire Fire and Rescue Service, and a special guest appearance from a first-team player such as Leroy Lita.

The Roadshow was extremely popular with teachers, parents and pupils alike. Community Manager Lee Herron said: "It's a great way of giving young fans access to the players whilst at the same time providing a serious educational message.

"ADT have been working very hard to make their sessions both interesting and informative, and the Berkshire Fire & Rescue Service's involvement has been another way of keeping the kids entertained and educated.

"The players have all enjoyed the sessions as well. At first a few of them were a bit daunted when they walked into a room full of 100 children, but we try to make sure it's a relaxed and friendly atmosphere, and by the end of the day it can be difficult to tear them away from all the photos and autographs!"

Neil Harrington, General Manager of ADT's Thames Valley branch, added, "Every week 20 schools in the UK are hit by potentially disastrous arson fires. The Royals Roadshow has proved to be a great way to promote fire safety at local schools and to raise greater awareness about this important issue."

A new version of the Roadshow will be launched in September 2007 – and this time the club has teamed up with Network Rail to create the 'Stop!' campaign which will educate children about safety around railway lines.